THE ACTUAL WORLD

Also by Jason Tandon

Quality of Life
Give Over the Heckler and Everyone Gets Hurt
Wee Hour Martyrdom

THE ACTUAL WORLD

JASON TANDON

To Ryan,
Here's to being
a local!

Cheers,

[signature]
10/19/19

Black
Lawrence
Press

.

www.blacklawrence.com

Executive Editor: Diane Goettel
Book Design: Amy Freels
Cover Design: Zoe Norvell

Published 2019 by Black Lawrence Press.
Printed in the United States.

for Charlie and Harper

Contents

My ambition is truly limited to a few clods of earth, some sprouting wheat.

—Vincent van Gogh

'I'm dime a dozen and so are you!'

—Arthur Miller

I

At the Orchard

We sit beneath a giant maple
watching pirouettes of yellow
gust upwards, each leaf
an illumined skin
stretched across a pliable spine.

My son spins an apple between his hands,
bites it like a buck-toothed animal.
Mouth full, cheeks juice-streaked
he laughs at the pig
wallowing in its mud pit.

Distantly I hear
the dull crunch of gravel
and I am a boy again
running down a dark road,
the sky full of stars
as if blown from an open palm.

When my father found me
at the edge of the reservoir
and shook my shoulders, angry and afraid,
I didn't know where
I was going. I didn't know why.

New England Sand & Gravel Co.

From beneath the stiff brim of an Irish flat cap
my neighbor hawks and spits
with the power of a pneumatic rifle.

The day we moved here
I waved to him. This morning
I smile. In black paint on a white board

the sign up the road says,
"We sell what we sell."

Sudden Death in Middle Age

When I heard that he'd had a heart attack
on a flight from Boston to Detroit
I went out to water the pots of sage
that flourish with little attention
on our west-facing stoop.

Straining to hear the water
seep through the soil, I saw an ant colony
migrating in multiple files
across the sidewalk.

On my hands and knees
what had looked like an organized march
was a frenzied mob of thousands
trampling one another
as if trapped inside a stadium riot—

the way that painting by Seurat
looks like a sunny day in the park,
crowds of people lounging
on the banks of a blue river,

but stand too close
and the images divide
into distinct dots of color
that dizzy the head and nauseate.

New Year's Day

All afternoon the snow has been falling
in flakes the size of silver dollars,
falling so slowly I can see
the crystalized patterns
of their intricate symmetry.

It piles on the shed roof
and against the chain-link,
windshield wipers like arms
shot up in surrender.

When it thins to a flurry
I will pull on my boots
as will we all on this block,
emerging like extras in the opening number
to heave and toss in rhythm.

On Turning Two

My son lowers his eyes
from the eagle hovering above us,
its wings fully spread
as if pinned to the azure sky—

jams his hand
the length of his arm
into the damp black spaces
between the jetty rocks.

What Jack Next Door Remembers about Vietnam

The explosion of the girl's nose.
The cracking orbital bones. Her spit
hitting a gold metal button on his uniform.
The pyramid of Wonder Bread on display,
the shine in her hair like a brushed mare's mane.
"Forgetting to buy the plates my dad
had forgotten for the party," he says,
and lifts a can of Natural Light
to kernels of boiled corn lodged in his gums.

After the Fourth

From the western shore
comes the annunciatory tremolo
of the common loon.
Then: no sounds

but the plash of bodies in the distant darkness
and the crescendo of a mosquito's
beating wings.

Waking on Vacation without Alarm

The kitchen
lit by the stove clock
a dungeon's
dank green,

I rub my spine
against the chair's
ladder back.

The hilltops
blush.

Genre

I did once write a love poem.
In it, a man sat on a park bench
so enraptured by the woman he loved
he didn't care about the sudden torrent of rain,
the mud spattering his new leather shoes.

I sent the poem in a letter,
then another letter
to confirm receipt of the first.
Finally, an envelope
sliced my mailbox in two.

And today, after a marriage,
the birth of a child, the deaths
of two dogs, the purchase of a house
and a second-hand couch,
its cushions sunk
from too many evenings of TV,
I heard she got divorced.

The Actual World

for Jane Kenyon

On the oiled grate of the kettle grill
the sausages split their skins, spurt
and hiss upon the coals.

I take a sip from my glass:
a mash of juniper and lemon,
angelica, coriander,
and grains of paradise

distilled with a neutral spirit
and poured with tonic
over ice.

Kindness

There it was, on Congress Street today,
a body limp and twisted
by a fender's curled metal.

Someone shouted, "Listen,"
and we heard a gurgling in the boy's throat,
we saw him raise a hand.

A man rocked the boy to his chest
despite the known command
to leave the injured where they lie

and pressed his ear to the boy's lips.
"I don't know it," the man said,
"I don't know the song."

A woman cradled the boy's face,
blood spitting into her eyes,
and began to sing a song

for which I knew the melody
but was feeling for the words,
my mouth moving in shapes

as the sirens drew nearer
and the drilling of a jackhammer
resumed.

Benign Paroxysmal Positional Vertigo

It was snowing on the lake.

I could not tell
where land ended,
where water began

and the line of the horizon seemed like
a smudged erasure
of pencil.

September

Children mill on corners
in bright clean clothing.
Arms akimbo, they grasp
the straps of their packs,

a rabble of colorful butterflies
swept into the school bus
by the slap
of its mechanical hand.

Cleaning House

In the picture I still keep
stashed in a sandwich bag
with a pack of Zig-Zags
and a sealed tin of Skoal,

her blond hair
has grown more brunette.

What I thought
was the end of beauty,
what kept me on the phone all night

was ordinary.

Having Forgotten to Put out Fresh Towels, I Run Naked and Wet to the Bedroom

In the amber glow of early morning
I see the dogwood's
silhouette
cast upon
the lowered shade.

Rolling and
unrolling the scroll

I don't know which
to prefer.

Dusk

for Charles Simic

The sky
a darkened ballroom,

someone hanging streamers
for the surprise.

Lines in Early Autumn

I drag my trash to the curb
as if tugging
a wayward dog.

The scrape
against the pavement
drowns out the crow
cawing from the shade tree.

At a Loss

What can I say to my friend up the street
who lost her baby boy
one day after his birth?
I script and rehearse.

There's a leak in my attic
down the chimney's face.
Grubs have browned the lawn.
Months go by.

At Thirty-Seven, I Hear the Cry of a Great Horned Owl for the First Time

As if at the thought of waking my wife—
a single branch
shudders.

In the Country

Suspended in this hammock
swaying in a shadow
between two pines,

eyes closed,
head emptying,

could you be content
oarless and adrift
on a vast, pitch-black sea?

II

Locker Room

Old men
so comfortable
in their skins.

Catharsis

It's amazing how
when I have an eyelash
beneath my contact lens
it feels like
I have a twig in my eye,
which is so unlike
an eyelash
in composition and size
it gives me greater perspective
on the pain and suffering
of Oedipus.

Discipline

You feel it coming.
An incommensurate anger.
The gesture your father made
like a butcher hacking through bone.

What must your face look like
for your son's to look like this?

There's no paddle. No switch.
When you're at the table
making noise with your peas,
you'll close your mouth. Beg pardon.

Early Morning in Late Summer

On-screen
rows of dead children
are laid against the vibrant geometry
of a Persian rug.

Their bodies are wrapped in white sheets,
twisted at each end
like taffy in waxed paper.
A few faces
are unwrapped. A girl's lips
are parted and blue.

On each chest
a torn piece of paper
has seemingly fallen

like a large flake of ash
from a burning book.

On the Dock

The setting sun
red and rippling

like a gunshot wound that can't be staunched.

Clumps of bloody gauze
                    litter the sky

as we nurse these beers
and dip our feet
into the clear
calm water.

I Was Having a Wonderful Dream

And woke to a wind
in the bare
winter trees.
I lay in bed

dozing to the creak of a harbored ship
straining
the anchor chain.

Moon Poem

after Harry Martinson

It hangs in the night sky
like a thumbnail—
the hand of God waving
to the other side of the earth.

Or perhaps the hand is elsewhere.
The opposite pole,
a parallel universe,

and this is a bit of His body
chewed off, spit out,
and lying on the bathroom tiles.

Calling for Intermittent Storms

A pan-fry wind
kicks up its sizzle,
blackens the leaves on the trees
as the sun disappears
and the booms draw nearer.

The masons chiseling slate
take another break
and pass around a cigarette
thick as a bone
and smelling of thyme, of sage.

A Dream of Departure

By the side of a dirt road
my father removed his pants
and threw them into an overgrown pasture.
My mother hung her stockings
over an electric fence.
There were others, all strangers,
like a tour group bound for Hawaii or Greece.
I began to ball the socks
clinging to the thistle.
The bus trumpeted. The door accordioned open.
"Please," my mother called, "leave the mess."

Paper Mill in Winter

The smoke billowing from its stacks
looks frozen in the air, like genies
half-emerged from their lamps,
their fat, prosperous bellies
stuck in the serpentine necks.

Self-Portrait: The Poet at Nine

In the courtyard's open air
I sit in a circle of women
shelling peas,

glancing between
the cut green mangoes
pickling in a jar

and the girl my age
squatting to sweep hose water
from a concrete floor.

April Foolishness

Back by the vending machines
you bled and you bled.
For three hours we waited
to confirm what you had felt

slip beneath the green fluorescence
of a public restroom.
"A clot," the nurse would call it.
"A clot," the doctor would repeat.

One week later, after a spell
of spring weather, it snowed again.
Enough to brush the car. The rest
I left for the eventual sun.

We had stowed our boots in the basement.
Washed our hats and jackets,
mittens and bibs,
and packed them with cedar
in a clear plastic bin.

After the Storm

Scarless
in a crepuscular calm,

the lake's
mirrored treescape
was a mosh of Gothic spires.

To the stone-cutter who asked,
"When will we finish?"
Gaudí replied,
"My client can wait."

Every day
he changed the plan.

Christmas Morning, after Illness

Down by the water
sitting cross-legged
on the bank,

the grass
white with frost,
bunched and lumpy
as an unmade bed,

I hear my son's voice
muffled, his hands
slapping glass:

Look at me, Daddy.
Daddy, look at me.

My Father at Seventy

Beyond the far shore
the winter hills, gray and barren—
"Not gray," my father says,
"not barren."

"See how the valleys of leafless trees
blur into purple,
and the pines
etch the ridges in blue."

He nods above the highest peak
cluttered with passing clouds.
"See the waning crescent moon."

L'Arabesque

for William B. Noto

In a small red room
off the kitchen
a man enters
the middle of his life.

His wife and son
are in the garden,
and he lifts his fingers
to the piano's yellowing keys.

In the silence that follows
he knows his left hand was heavy,
his sixteenth notes uneven.

He feels the spade
rasping in the loam,
the floors of his heart flooding.

[December snow.]

December snow.
The sparrows peck
what the cardinal spilled.

Beatitude

Out of oil
on a cold Sunday morning
we heap the bed with blankets.

I Looked up to See

Gathering twigs
blown from a neighbor's
dying elm

I looked up to see
a caterpillar
suspended in the air.

It hung by a strand of silk
visible
as a glint of white light

only when
the caterpillar
hoisted
itself.

Picnic

The kids come back
when they are called.
When they are called
the kids come back.

The kids come back
when they are called.
When they are called
the kids come back.

Between Poems

Inside the cage of its claws
a squirrel whittles an oak nut

until the yellow meat shines
like a nugget of gold.

Cairns of shell shards
pile on a plank of the aluminum dock.

       *

Sunlight jabs
through the muscled bulk of the flexing clouds
scattering a fistful of pennies
                         across the water.

Wading to my waist
in the bracing cold, my pockets inflate.

III

Still Life

after Derain

The basket is empty.
No bread, no wheel of cheese.
No milk in the pitcher,
no wine in the glass.

But the white dish is full
of plump green grapes,
a ripe peach. The pears
he's painted black.

Shadows cross the table
like a devil's spindly fingers
stealing towards the sugar
and the salt.

I'm sorry. The shadows
are just shadows,
faithfully rendered.
The devil? Forgive me.

Morning Commute

We rise in darkness,
rain falling
like crystal splinters
from a smashed chandelier,

knowing soon
the red shoots of the peonies
will spear through the mulch,
the ants will burrow above the frost line,

the mothers and fathers of those massacred children
will bend to the hyacinth,
a black horse at its trough.

The Retreat

for Justin F. A. Racz

When the heat went out
and the phone
died on its cradle

we drove past the hum of a winch
and a compressor's
hydraulic sigh

to where stars blued in the night
like chips of glacial ice.

In the glow of an open stove
we sat at a table
large and lacquered

and the plate we passed between us
seemed as if it were
slowly drifting

across a still river.

The Reminder

My friend long dead visits me in a dream.
"You've married," he says, "you've had a child."
"Yes," I say, feeling my face flush with shame.
"I grieved for you," I say. "I climbed a rooftop
in a slanting rain and spit my curses at God."
He smiles, and the rows of his teeth appear
like spotless glasses brimming with milk.

Morning Commute

My wife's body
rolled on its side
is a shadowy hill,

our son
curled at the foot.
His breathing,
radio static—

a match flare
in each lung.

The Book

A new book
long awaited

finally arrives.
Its cover

is bent and stained.
It is also

the wrong book.
I learn

to live with it.

The Engine Has Stalled

And here we are
in the middle of the bay,

the evening sun
like an egg
cracked on the mountain range,

the broken yolk
sliding towards
a couple bits of burnt fat.

Memory

A cotton bra
snagged on the knob of a fallen tree
that lies across a frigid river,

left by a pair of teenaged lovers
who dashed
at the flickering sweep
of a bored patrolman's spotlight.

He Must Be Tired

My neighbor's grass
uncut for a month,

the tip of each blade
glistening with a dewdrop

that flares bright white
in the rising sun,

a throng of sweaty fans
begging

for another song.

Visiting a Friend Who Was Given Six Months to Live Eleven Years Ago

He carved the venison into thick pink slices,
poured the wine
and took my hand in prayer.

Wading out to Tarp the Boat on My Fortieth Birthday

Rods of yellow light
poke through
a dark swath of low-lying clouds,

an unseen hand
placing candles
in a perfect circle.

Thanksgiving

I wake alone,
the house
full of family,

the kids
humped above the blankets

like fish
leaping from the sea.

Directive

Do not open
the catalogue of your failures.
Loss is not the occasion here.

In the gray-white light
of a winter dawn, see
the obese jogger

scuff the road, exhausted.

Swimming Alone in Broad Bay

From beneath the black water
the boat that cuts its engine
sounds like a circular saw
jamming in a plank of knotty pine,
or like the father who gives up
telling his son what is best.

Matrimony

We lie naked above the sheets
watching the curtains
robe the wind.

Later, in the splotch
of the small hours
I tell you,
"We're low on dish soap."

You answer,
"Coffee, too."

Weekend Away

for Robert Bly

Rising
from roadside gullies,

the culvert's
            rippled spillage,

mayflies
glut the lake.

        *

We dive.

The Last Time I Cried

It was the end of August,
a Tuesday, I think.
The sky had warmed a soft
baby blue, save for a stubborn cloud
the color of roadside snow.

Early Morning, Spring

Inside the house
my mother is waking
in the same white nightgown
she wore when I was a child.

Her hair has turned white
as if blanched suddenly
and the half-moons beneath her eyes
are creviced and pale.

At pond's edge
I watch an insect paddle its oars
to a mass of jellied frogspawn

and in a pocket
of lingering winter air,
feel the ropes of my shoulders loosen.

Then

Somewhere there is music playing.
A light is on. Someone is pouring drinks.

Here, there is a table.
A candle
sputtering in its melt.

The stars,
a bag of feed
torn and trailing in the sky.

Acknowledgments

I am grateful to the editors and staffs of the following publications in which some of these poems first appeared, often in earlier versions:

AGNI Online: "Having Forgotten to Put out Fresh Towels, I Run Naked and Wet to the Bedroom," "I Looked up to See"

The Alembic: "I Was Having a Wonderful Dream," "Matrimony," "September"

Barrow Street: "Weekend Away"

Beloit Poetry Journal: "Discipline"

Burnside Review: "Benign Paroxysmal Positional Vertigo"

Chicago Quarterly Review: "Visiting a Friend Who Was Given Six Months to Live Eleven Years Ago"

Cold Mountain Review: "After the Fourth," "On the Dock"

Folio: "Still Life"

Gargoyle: "Lines in Early Autumn," "Locker Room," "Memory"

The Journal: "At Thirty-Seven, I Hear the Cry of a Great Horned Owl for the First Time," "The Book"

Lake Effect: "Directive," "Dusk," "Early Morning, Spring," "The Retreat"

The Laurel Review: "The Engine Has Stalled," "Moon Poem"

The Louisville Review: "My Father at Seventy"

Modern Haiku: "[December snow.]"

Mudfish: "Morning Commute (We rise in darkness)," "Thanksgiving"

Natural Bridge: "Calling for Intermittent Storms"

New Madrid: "New England Sand & Gravel Co."

Passages North: "Paper Mill in Winter," "Then"

Paterson Literary Review: "Cleaning House"

Poet Lore: "The Actual World," "Kindness," "Morning Commute (My wife's body)," "Wading out to Tarp the Boat on My Fortieth Birthday"

Poetry East: "Early Morning in Late Summer," "In the Country," "L'Arabesque," "New Year's Day," "Sudden Death in Middle Age," "Swimming Alone in Broad Bay"

RHINO: "April Foolishness"

Ruminate: "A Dream of Departure," "At a Loss," "Christmas Morning, after Illness"

The Saint Ann's Review: "After the Storm" (originally published as "Praise"), "Catharsis"

Salamander: "At the Orchard"

The Southampton Review: "Beatitude"

The South Carolina Review: "Genre"

Spillway: "Self-Portrait: The Poet at Nine"

SRPR (Spoon River Poetry Review): "What Jack Next Door Remembers about Vietnam"

Tar River Poetry: "On Turning Two"

Water~Stone Review: "Between Poems," "The Reminder"

Photo: Kishan N. Tandon

Jason Tandon is the author of four books of poetry, including *Quality of Life*, *Wee Hour Martyrdom*, and *Give Over the Heckler and Everyone Gets Hurt*, winner of the St. Lawrence Book Award from Black Lawrence Press. His poems have appeared in *Ploughshares*, *Prairie Schooner*, *Beloit Poetry Journal*, *AGNI Online*, *Barrow Street*, and *Esquire*, among others. He earned his B.A. and M.A. from Middlebury College, and his M.F.A. from the University of New Hampshire. Since 2008, he has taught in the Arts & Sciences Writing Program at Boston University.